Kimberly is a Board-Certified Behaviour Analyst and has spent most of her career working with special needs students in San Diego, California for private companies, the public school system as well as her own self founded company, running social skills groups for people of all ages and abilities.

Through her work, she has found that learned coping strategies are one of the key foundational skills for teaching self-regulation to students, to help decrease maladaptive behaviours, no matter their age. She hopes that reading *Calming Is as Easy as 1, 2, 3!* with your child will teach them to practice and learn coping strategies that they can use every day!

Calming is as Easy as

1, 2, 3!

Kimberly Siroky

AUSTIN MACAULEY PUBLISHERS™
LONDON • CAMBRIDGE • NEW YORK • SHARJAH

A CIP catalogue record for this title is available from the British Library.

ISBN 9781398465589 (Paperback)
ISBN 9781398465596 (ePub e-book)

www.austinmacauley.com

First Published 2023
Austin Macauley Publishers Ltd®
1 Canada Square
Canary Wharf
London
E14 5AA

To my wonderful talented illustrator, Declan, and all of my former students, for constantly amazing me. And to my brilliant and handsome son, Grady, for inspiring me daily to reach for my dreams.

Thank you to my mom for instilling a love of reading and writing in me from a young age and to my supportive and loving husband for encouraging me to become an author.

Watching TV and playing games is always lots of fun, but when Mom and Dad say, "That's enough," play time for now, is done.

Declan is mad, he doesn't want to clean his room,
video games are so much more fun!

Help him calm by counting out loud... 1 to 10 or like
an astronaut, 10 to 1!

Piper wants a new bear but Mom says "no"… Before she can say "next time dear", Piper begins to scream, and loudly I fear!

When we don't get our way, it's okay to be a little sad. Help Piper take deep breaths, so she doesn't feel so mad!

Start in the middle, deep breathing can be fun!
Breathe in on the right loop, out on the next, just three more times and then you are done!

Sometimes friends can be mean or cruel but you can make the right choice if you follow the rules!

Help Piper calm her body down rather than
kick or scream.

When you stretch your arms and legs having fun,
you made a good choice it seems!

When learning new things is hard and you want to cry, just ask for a break to keep your eyes dry!

Declan can't decide how to spend his break...
fresh air, deep breaths...
read a book or close his eyes?

You can spin a wheel or roll some dice! Any choice
is the right one, its as easy as pie!

Accidents happen all the time, we get hurt and it makes us cry – that's okay, what's important is that we tried!

If you're sad and need to be alone, make a quiet space that's just for you... you can even invite your favorite toys and a soft blanky too!

Piper had her bath, now the sun is gone...
she sees her pup Spot, ooh a book and toy bear!
For her, play time is not done!

"Bedtime dear," says Mom and Dad.
"Nooooo," she cries out – that was not what
she wanted to hear!

When we get upset and want to yell and pout, take some sips of water - just put your cup under the spout!

Help Piper calm before bed by filling up her cup at the sink, then all she has to do is slowly take a drink!

The End!

Printed in the USA
CPSIA information can be obtained
at www.ICGtesting.com
LVHW060856250124
769813LV00077B/2399